# PATRIOTISM

Pride in your country's achievements is an important part of patriotism.

THE VALUES LIBRARY

# PATRIOTISM

Linda Carlson Johnson

THE ROSEN PUBLISHING GROUP, INC.

NEW YORK

Published in 1990, 1993 by The Rosen Publishing Group, Inc.
29 East 21st Street, New York NY 10010

**Revised Edition, 1993**
Copyright © 1990, 1993 by The Rosen Publishing Group, Inc.

Printed in the United States of America

**Library of Congress Cataloging-in Publication Data**

Johnson, Linda Carlson, 1948–
    Patriotism / Linda Carlson Johnson.
    (The Values library)
    Includes bibliographical references and index.
    Summary: Examines the concept of patriotism, discussing its many forms, symbols,
and meanings.
    ISBN 0-8239-1507-7
    1. Patriotism—Juvenile literature. [1. Patriotism.] I. Title. II. Series.
JC326.J65   1990
323,6'.5—dc20                                                          89-37109
                                                                            CIP
                                                                            AC

# C O N T E N T S

# INTRODUCTION

ON THE EVENING OF AUGUST 6, 1992, Carl Lewis stood on the winner's platform in the middle of a track in Barcelona, Spain. He had just won a gold medal in the long-jump competition for the third Olympics in a row.

For Carl Lewis, three gold-medal performances in three straight Olympics was an amazing and unique victory. But Carl Lewis's medal was a great achievement for more than just Carl Lewis. It was also a triumph for his homeland: the United States of America.

As the track star stood on the highest tier of the awards platform, *The Star-Spangled Banner* played on the loudspeaker to a sold-out crowd of spectators from all over the world. As America's national anthem played, the American flag was slowly raised up—along with the flags of the silver- and bronze-medal winners—but the American flag

## Love and pride for your country are parts of a feeling called patriotism.

was raised the highest. For that moment, the accomplishments of Carl Lewis brought honor to America in front of the entire world. And Americans who saw the awards that night felt a special proud feeling for their country as well. That special feeling is patriotism.

Americans were not the only ones who were proud that night in Barcelona. The Olympic Games give every country in the world an opportunity to excel and gain honor. Every athlete that competes in an Olympics is, in a way, a special ambassador for his or her country. And the triumphs and failures of an Olympic athlete are also the triumphs and failures of his and her country.

Each athlete becomes the focus of patriotism for the citizens of his or her homeland. Representing your country in front of the entire world is a great responsibility. But it is also a unique opportunity to show your love for your country—your patriotism—and to bring honor to your nation and all the people who live within it.

This book will help you to understand what patriotism is—and what it is not. It will also help you to take a closer look at what your country means to you.

In the Olympic Games, athletes compete against each other and represent the countries where they live.

# 1

# WHAT IS PATRIOTISM?

*It is time for a big race at the Olympic Games. Runners from 10 countries take off at top speed. The crowd cheers wildly. The top three runners cross the finish line. After the race, they climb up on stands and wave to the crowd. The winner is a runner from Kenya, a country in Africa. He is on the highest stand. A judge puts a gold medal around his neck as the crowd cheers again. Then some music begins, and the crowd becomes silent. Everyone stands and listens as the national song of Kenya plays. At one end of the stadium, the flag of Kenya goes up. The runner from Kenya keeps his eyes on the flag. Tears are running down his cheeks. Many people from Kenya are in the crowd. They have tears in their eyes too.*

**THE RUNNER FROM KENYA CRIES BECAUSE HE IS HAPPY.** He is happy because he won the race. But he is also happy because he won the race for his country. He loves his country. He feels proud when he hears his country's song and

Abebe Bikila of Ethiopia won the Olympic Marathon in 1960, setting a world record.

watches his country's flag go up. The people from Kenya who are in the crowd feel proud and happy, too.

There is a word that describes the feeling the runner and the people from Kenya have for their country. The word is *patriotism*. Patriotism is a strong love of country. It is the kind of love that makes people want to do things for their country.

Competing in the Olympic Games is one thing a person can do for his or her country. But very few people have the talent to win those kinds of contests. Everyone has what it takes to be a patriot, though.

You do not have to be a great athlete to be a patriot. You do not have to be famous. You do not have to do anything out of the ordinary.

Every good citizen in every country is a patriot. Patriots care what their government is doing. They try to do things to make their country a better place to live. They feel proud of their country. They don't do things that will hurt their country.

Why do people have such strong feelings about their country? They have these feelings because their countries are their homes. They feel that the other people in their countries are like members of their families.

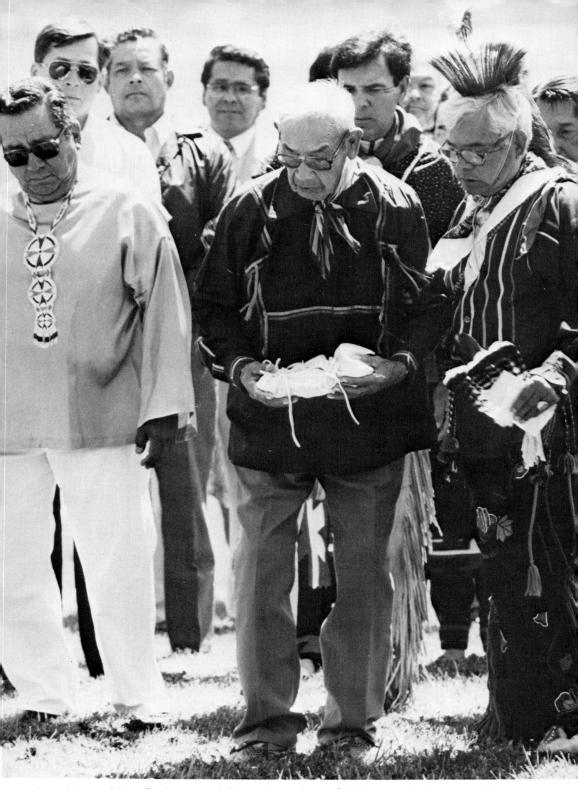

An elder of the Delaware tribe of western Oklahoma takes part in a native American ceremony.

# 2

---

# THE ROOTS OF PATRIOTISM

**CHILDREN ARE NOT BORN WITH A LOVE OF COUNTRY.** When children are small, they can't understand the idea that they live in a country. They can't even understand that they live in a town or a neighborhood. Small children know only about a very small world: their home.

To small children, home is a place where everything is familiar and safe. In their homes, most children are cared for by people who love them. From a very young age, children understand that they belong in this group called a *family.*

What do children learn in a family? They learn family stories that have been passed down through the years. They learn their family's *traditions,* too. For example, children learn about special foods their families like to have for holiday meals. Children learn from their parents about love. They learn that people who love one another want to do things for one another. Children also learn that family members can count on one another in good times and in bad times.

**"In love of home, love of country has its rise."**

—*Charles Dickens*

---

In places such as school and church, children widen the circle of people who are important to them. They make friends with other children. Kids who become friends tell each other all about their lives. They learn to do things together and to do things for each other. They also learn that friends, like family members, stick by each other in good times and in bad times.

This feeling that you will stick by a person or group of people, no matter what happens, is called *loyalty*. You probably feel loyalty toward your family and friends. You may feel a sense of loyalty to your school, too. This feeling of school loyalty is called school "spirit."

If you have been a member of a sports team, you probably know about team spirit too. When you put on a team uniform, you are saying that you are part of the team. You feel pride in your team's uniform and name. Even if you're not playing, you root for your team. You try to do your best for your team because other people are depending on you. You don't quit the team, even if it's losing. When your team wins, the whole team cheers at once. It's the *team* that wins, not just you.

You learn about loyalty by being a part of a family, a group of friends, or a team. Patriotism is another kind of loyalty—loyalty to country. People who are patriots feel as if they are members of a large family of people who form a nation. Many people call their country a fatherland, a motherland, or a homeland. The word *patriot* comes from a word that means "father."

Patriots feel a strong sense of love and loyalty to their homeland. They care about their homeland so much that they are willing to do their best to serve it. And they are willing to stand by their country, no matter what.

Loyalty to a group comes from a feeling of belonging to that group.

# 3

## SYMBOLS OF PATRIOTISM

REMEMBER THE RUNNER FROM KENYA WHO WON the race in the Olympics? Why did he cry? He didn't cry just because he was happy. He cried because he was proud to win for his country. His country's song and his country's flag brought tears to his eyes.

Every country has a special song called a national anthem. This anthem is a song that everyone in the country knows. The song has words that tell about the country. Patriotic people stand up when they sing the national anthem. Even if they do not sing, they stand quietly while the song plays.

Every country has a flag, too. A flag is just a piece of colorful cloth, but it is very important to the people of a country. People stand up when their flag goes by. They may place their hands over their hearts or even salute as the flag is raised. Soldiers carry their country's flag into battle. Mountain climbers carry their country's flag with

16

When the national anthem is played people show respect for their country. If they are sitting, they stand while the anthem plays. They may place their right hands over their hearts as a gesture of respect.

> *"Hats off! The flag is passing by!"*
> —*Henry Holcomb Bennett*

them. When they reach the top of a mountain, they put their country's flag there. Explorers carry their country's flag, too. When they reach a new land, they put their country's flag there. Space explorers do the same thing. American astronauts were the first space explorers to stand on the moon. People all over the world watched as they put the flag of the United States on the moon.

The flag and the national song of a country are *symbols* of a country. A *symbol* is something that *stands for* something else. So a flag or a song *stands for* a country. When people hear their national song or see their flag, they feel patriotic about their country. There are many other patriotic symbols, too.

### An animal can stand for a country.

What country comes to mind when you think of a kangaroo? Australia, of course.

### A building, a statue, or even a wall can stand for a country.

- A place called the Bastille is an important symbol to the French people. The Bastille was once a prison in Paris, France. Just over 200 years ago, the French people went to war against the king. The people wanted to rule the country themselves. During the war, called the French Revolution, the people took over the Bastille. So the Bastille became a symbol of freedom from the king. Today, the French people celebrate Bastille Day.

• The Statue of Liberty stands for freedom in the U.S. The Statue of Liberty is a huge statue of a woman. It stands in New York City harbor. The woman holds a torch high over her head. For many years, when people came to the U.S. from other countries by boat, the statue was the first thing they saw. The statue seemed to welcome them to their new home. It was a symbol of the freedom they hoped to find in their new land.

• The Great Wall is a symbol to the people of China. This wall stretches for 1500 miles along the northern border of China, one of the biggest countries in the world. The wall was built to protect China against enemies. It is a symbol of the strength of the Chinese people. It also stands for China as a proud country that doesn't need help from any other country in the world. Today, some people in China would like the Great Wall to be torn down. These people believe that China does need help from other countries in the world. They think that the Great Wall says to other countries, "Stay out of China."

Astronauts planted the United States' flag on the moon.

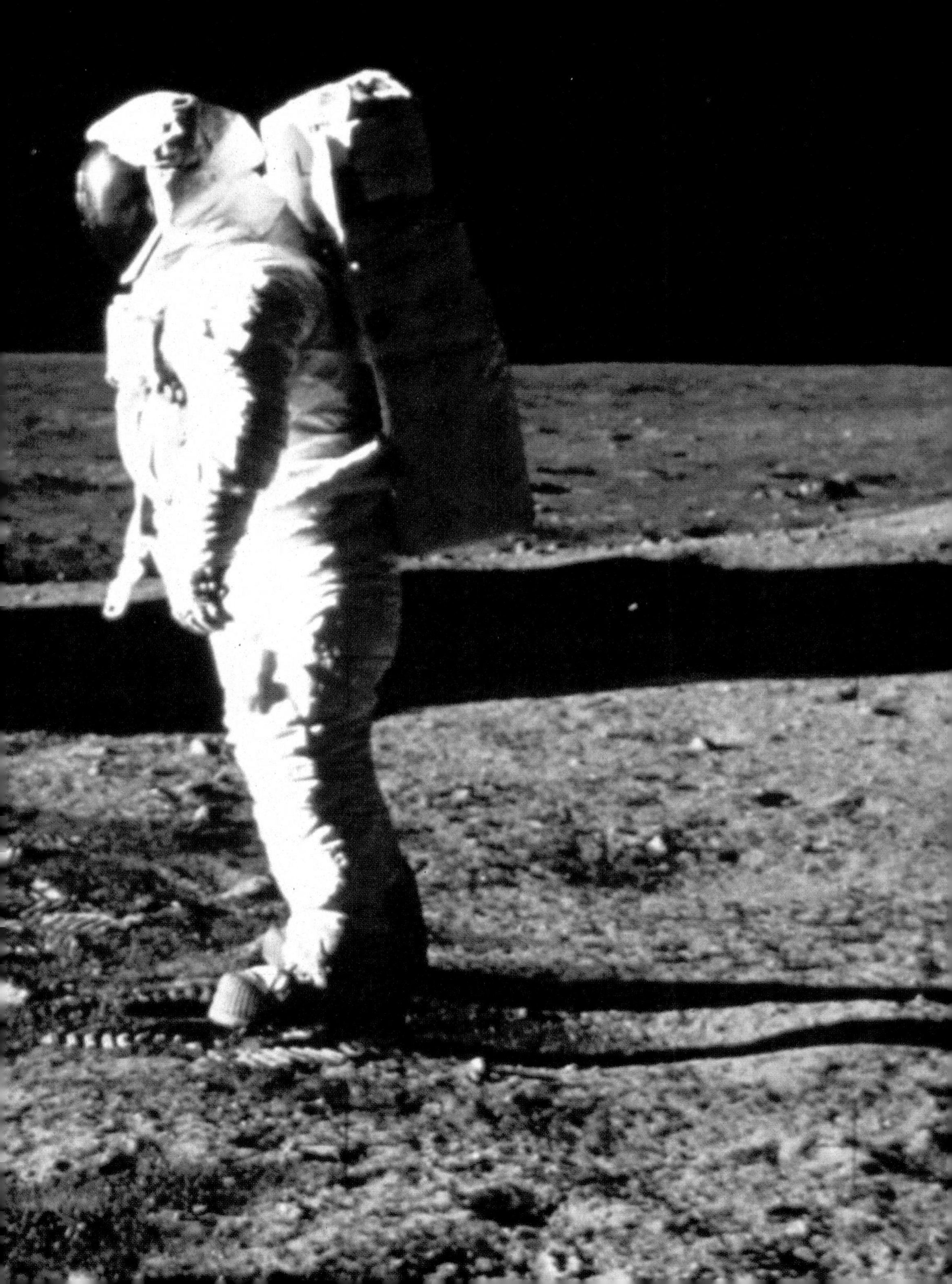

The maple leaf is the symbol of Canada.

**Something as simple as a leaf can stand for a country.**

In Canada, the leaf of a maple tree is a symbol of the country. There are many maple trees in Canada. The maple leaf reminds the people of Canada of how beautiful their country is. But the maple leaf is a symbol in another way. The maple leaf has one stem but many parts. The parts of the leaf stand for the parts of Canada. The leaf is a symbol that shows how many different parts of the country work together.

**Other songs besides a country's national song can be symbols for a country.**

For example, when people hear the song "Danny Boy," they think of Ireland.

**People can be symbols of patriotism, too.**

In England, the queen does not rule the country. People are elected to do that. But the queen is still very important to the people. People like to hear about the queen and her family. The queen stands for the country of England. In fact, England's national anthem is called, "God Save the Queen."

What are the symbols of patriotism in your country?

Colonists fought the British in the American Revolution.

# 4

## PATRIOTS ALL

**SOME PATRIOTS ARE PEOPLE WHOSE NAMES** have become world-famous because of their deeds. Some patriots are well known, but only in their own countries. Some patriots are people whose names are never recorded in history books. But they all have one thing in common—they have put their countries' best interests before their own needs. Here are stories of some patriots from past and present.

• George Washington was a famous patriot of the American Revolution. He was chief of the American army during a war in which the American colonies broke away from England, the country that had ruled them for over a century. After the colonies won the war, George Washington became the first president of the new country, which was called the United States. A man who spoke at George Washington's funeral called him "the father of his country." The man said George Washington was "first in war, first in peace, and first in the hearts of his countrymen."

"The really patriotic citizen is the one who loves."

*— Cardinal Hayes*

---

More than 200 years after George Washington died, people in the United States still remember him as one of the nation's greatest patriots.

• A girl named Phyllis Wheatley lived in America during the same period that George Washington lived there. Today, few Americans know who Phyllis Wheatley was. But she was a great patriot, too.

Phyllis came to America from Africa as a slave. She was owned by the Wheatley family, who gave her their name. Mrs. Wheatley taught Phyllis to speak, read, and write English. When Phyllis was a teenager, she began writing poems. Phyllis wrote a special poem during the American Revolution. It was about George Washington and the love Phyllis had for her new country. George liked the poem so much that he asked to meet Phyllis.

Phyllis was the first African American poet. And she was a patriot.

• Golda Meir became famous as a patriot. Like George Washington, she played an important part in starting a new country.

Golda Meir was born in Russia in 1898. She was a Jew. As a small child, she saw Russian soldiers arrest and kill many Jews. Later, Golda's family moved to the United

Paul Revere warned the colonists that the British were going to attack.

Phyllis Wheatley was the first African American poet. She wrote of her love for her new country.

States, where she grew up. Golda liked the United States, but she remembered what happened to the Jews. She believed there should be a country that Jews could call home. She left the United States and moved to Palestine, where many Jewish people lived. Golda lived there for many years. Then World War II came. Six million Jews were arrested and killed by the Germans in Europe. Golda worked even harder for a Jewish homeland. She raised millions of dollars, and she continued to speak out. Finally a new country for Jewish people was born in 1948. That country is Israel. Golda Meir became one of the first leaders of Israel.

• In a country far from Israel, a young man who was a patriot risked his life because he cared about freedom for his people. No one knows this young man's name. No one perhaps even remembers his face. They just remember what he did.

This young patriot's homeland is China. China is a country that is ruled by the Communist party. The leaders of China do not allow people to speak out against the government. But in 1989, some Chinese students wanted to tell their government that they wanted more freedom. The students sat in the middle of Tiananmen Square in the city of Beijing. They said they would not eat until the government listened to them.

Golda Meir helped found the state of Israel in 1948.

While the students fasted, millions of citizens traveled to Tiananmen Square. The world waited to see what the Chinese government would do. Finally, the government gave its answer. Army troops moved in and began shooting. Many people in the square were killed.

One news photo from Tiananmen Square tells the story of the people's struggle. It is the photo of a young man standing alone in front of a column of government tanks. Few people even know this young patriot's name. But his bravery will be remembered.

Chinese students protested for freedom in June, 1989.

Sometimes patriotism means fighting or dying for your country.

# 5

# NO PRICE IS TOO HIGH

**NATHAN HALE'S FAMOUS LAST WORDS WERE,** " I regret that I have but one life to lose for my country." He said that just after a British soldier put a noose around his neck. A few seconds later, the soldier kicked away the ladder Nathan was standing on. Nathan dropped quickly, as his neck broke.

During the American Revolution, Nathan was captured by the British. He would not tell the British what he knew. He said, "Nothing could make me turn traitor to my country." He meant that nothing the British could do would make him turn against his country.

At 21 years of age, Nathan Hale had paid the highest price for patriotism. He had paid for his love of country with his life. Many other patriots in history have been willing to fight for their countries, even though it meant they might be thrown in prison or die.

> **"I realize I am a marked man, but if they kill or arrest me, someone else is ready to take my place."**
>
> *—Vaclav Havel*

---

• A priest named Miguel Hidalgo y Costillo was an important patriot in Mexico. Mexico had been ruled by Spain for a long time. But Hidalgo and many others wanted Mexico to be free. Hidalgo began the fight against Spain when he rang the church bells in a village called Dolores. That was in 1810. For the next year, Hidalgo led about 80,000 men in a war against the Spanish. Hidalgo lost his fight. He was captured and shot to death in 1811. But others kept fighting. Finally, in 1822, Mexico won its war against Spain. People in Mexico call Hidalgo "the father of Mexican independence."

• Vaclav Havel had been born into a rich family in Czechoslovakia, but when communists took over his country, all his family's wealth was taken away. The government didn't allow Vaclav to go to college, so he taught himself. He became a writer of plays and poems. He was thrown into prison many times because his wrote things the government didn't like. He could have left the country, but he decided to stay. "Only by staying here and struggling here can we ever hope to change things," he said. Havel knew he could be killed, but he kept fighting for decades. Finally, in 1990, the communist government fell. Vaclav Havel, poet and patriot, became the first president of a free Czechoslovakia.

• A young girl who could not read or write became a famous patriot in France. Her name was Joan of Arc. When

Joan of Arc was a young French girl who led her country's army in a war with England.

Joan was just a teenager, she saw a bright light and heard the voice of angels. She said the voices told her to lead the French soldiers in a war against England. Many people thought Joan was crazy. But then one captain listened to Joan. He let Joan lead the soldiers in battle. She was hurt several times and later captured by the English. She was tied to a stake and burned alive. Joan of Arc was willing to die for her country.

Patriots often love their country so much that they will do almost anything for it. But can patriots do too much?

In Germany during the 1930s, the Hitler Youth terrorized the Jews
in the name of patriotism. Books written by Jews were collected
and burned.

# 6

# IN THE NAME OF PATRIOTISM

**"HEIL HITLER!" WAS THE CRY** of many German people during World War II. People said these words to show that they believed in their leader, Adolf Hitler. Some of the people who said these words were children.

Many German children joined groups of Hitler Youth. The children learned about Hitler's ideas in these groups. One of the things they learned was to report anyone who spoke out against Hitler. Some children learned this lesson very well. They reported their own parents to the police. Sometimes the children's parents were killed or put in prison by the police for speaking against Hitler.

Were these children patriots? If you had asked them, they would have said yes. But what they did in the name of patriotism was terrible.

Halfway across the world, soldiers were killing themselves in the name of patriotism. These men flew planes for Japan during World War II. They had been taught that it was an honor to die for the emperor of Japan. So they became kamikaze pilots. Each kamikaze pilot knew he would die. His job was to crash his plane into a ship. That way he could kill hundreds of his enemies. Each kamikaze pilot wanted a chance to die that way.

In any war, many soldiers are willing to die for their country. But they do not usually do it on purpose. The kamikaze pilots of Japan died in the name of patriotism. They were heroes to many Japanese people. But were they true patriots?

Many things are done in the name of patriotism. The people who do these things say they are patriots. Yet other people do not agree that they are patriots.

People have committed crimes and even killed in the name of patriotism. You might say, "I would never do anything like that!" You probably wouldn't. But most of the people who have done wrong things in the name of patriotism probably thought they never would do these things either.

Being a patriot does not mean blindly following the leaders of your country. As a patriot, it is your job to *think*, not just to follow. You already have strong feelings about right and wrong. When you are asked to do something that you know is wrong, an alarm goes off inside your head. Listen to that alarm. It's up to you as a citizen and

Japanese *kamikaze* pilots flew suicide missions during World War II. They felt it was an honor to die for their country.

patriot to let your leaders know when you feel that something they are asking you to do is wrong.

You should love your country. But you should not do something that you feel is wrong in the name of your country. Part of being a patriot is doing the *right* thing.

In the early part of the 20th century, women had to fight to get the vote.

# 7

# FIGHTING FOR WHAT IS RIGHT

**THE WORDS "OUR COUNTRY, RIGHT OR WRONG"** have been used to tell people that they should go along with whatever their government says to do. But when a United States Senator said these words in 1872, he meant something very different. He meant that patriots should fight for what is right or good. And they should fight against what is wrong or bad.

Even in a free country, that fight is not always easy. In the United States, women and blacks had to fight for the right to vote. They won that right. But it took a long time, and it was hard work.

In a country that is not free, the fight for what is right is much harder. The Soviet Union was a Communist country for most of the 20th century. The government ruled the country by fear. People who spoke out against the government were often killed. Many were arrested and put in prison camps.

*41*

**"Our country, right or wrong. When right, to
be kept right; when wrong, to be put right."**
—*Carl Schurz*

---

In 1985, things began to change in the Soviet Union as
a new leader, Mikhail Gorbachev, came to power.
Gorbachev allowed more freedom for the Soviet people.
Soon, the people of Lithuania, a republic located along the
Baltic Sea, voted to break away from the Soviet Union to
be free of Soviet control altogether. Lithuania had been a
separate country before World War II.

The Soviet government's answer to Lithuania's vote for
independence was to send tanks to the capital, Vilnius.
Soviet soldiers attacked and shut down the TV station.
Tanks surrounded the capitol building. But the leaders of
Lithuania would not give up their fight for freedom. They
stayed inside the capitol building for months.

The leaders of Lithuania knew that they were risking
their lives to keep up their fight. But they kept on. Finally,
in 1991, Lithuania won its struggle. Lithuania was once
again a free nation!

Many other Soviet republics were struggling for freedom, too. Three brave Slavic leaders met to declare the
end of the Union of Soviet Socialist Republics (USSR). One
of these patriots was Boris Yeltsin, the Russian republic
president. Yeltsin worked hard to establish "democratic
legal states."

On December 21, 1991, representatives from eleven
former Soviet republics signed an agreement to create the

Lech Walesa is a Polish patriot and leader of the Solidarity movement.

Commonwealth of Independent States. The end of the Soviet Union was certain.

In another nation, Poland, a man named Lech Walesa helped his country win its freedom from Communist rule.

During the late 1970s and early 1980s, many of Poland's trade unions that were not controlled by the government, began an important movement. They wanted Poland's Communist government to listen to their ideas. They wanted to make Poland a better place to work and live.

Lech Walesa was an electrician in the now-famous Gdansk shipyards in Poland. As leader of this "Solidarity" movement, he became a world-wide symbol of patriotism and peace. He promised to fight for higher pay and more

political freedom for everyone in Poland. He promised to
try to make the government work hard to solve the
country's many problems.

At first, the government listened to Lech Walesa and the
members of Solidarity. But as the movement grew, the
government became afraid. Lech Walesa and others were
put in prison for a while. The Solidarity movement was
outlawed. But the people did not give up.

In 1983, Lech Walesa was awarded the Nobel Peace
Prize for his work. Walesa helped to keep the Solidarity
movement alive. He and others worked to make things
better for everyone in Poland. He traveled all over the
world for his cause. Solidarity members did not believe in
violence. They struggled peacefully to gain rights and
freedoms. After Communism fell, Walesa became one of
the first leaders of a free Poland.

Walesa and the people of the former Soviet republics
did not like what was happening in their countries. They
fought for change.

There are many patriots in the world today fighting for
what is right in their countries. Some of them must fight in
dangerous ways. But other patriots fight for what is right
quietly. They vote on election day. They write to newspapers. They go to meetings and say what they think. They
let their voices be heard.

# 8

## NATIONS BAND TOGETHER

**THE PEOPLE OF A COUNTRY SHARE THEIR FEELING OF PRIDE,** their patriotism, in their nation. But people are part of larger communities, too. Sometimes, the people of many nations band together to fight injustice or to work for peace.

In many of the nations of the Middle East, people share a common background. They are Arabs who speak the same language, Arabic, and practice the same religion, Islam. The Arab nations have a long tradition of standing up for one another against other nations. But in 1990, something happened that caused the Arab nations to ask for help from other nations.

Saddam Hussein, the leader of the Arab nation of Iraq, wanted the oil and wealth of Kuwait, a tiny Arab country that borders Iraq. Iraq's army stormed into Kuwait and took over the country. Saddam Hussein also threatened to take over Saudi Arabia, another Arab country on Kuwait's border.

*45*

What would Saudi Arabia and the other Arab nations do? Some Arab leaders argued that this problem was just an Arab problem and should be settled among the Arab nations. But other leaders didn't agree. They said the Arab nations should call for help from the United Nations (U.N.).

The king of Saudi Arabia did ask for help from the U.N. The U.N. Security Council voted to condemn the action of Saddam Hussein. And the Council said that if Saddam Hussein didn't get out of Kuwait, the U.N. would allow other nations to use force to push him out.

Saddam Hussein refused to leave Kuwait, and the Persian Gulf War began. The forces of many nations, led by the United States, attacked Saddam Hussein's forces in Kuwait. Arab military forces joined in the fight against Iraq, too. In just two months, the war was over. Saddam Hussein's army was forced back into Iraq.

In the Persian Gulf War, many nations of the world joined forces to fight against injustice. Nations band together for many other reasons, too.

• **Nations help each other in times of disaster.** For example, in 1991, several huge storms hit Bangladesh, a country in Asia. The people of many other nations sent medicine, food, and supplies. When widespread famine hit Somalia, a country in eastern Africa, many nations again tried to help. They sent food by the planeload.

It is patriotic to exercise your rights as a citizen. The right to vote is one of the most important. It gives you a voice in your government.

**"...I love human nature better than my country."**

*—Telanique*

---

• **Nations agree to fight pollution and damage to the environment.** Many nations of Europe agreed that their factories would stop producing certain gases that cause *acid rain*, for example. (Acid rain is rain that contains harmful chemicals it picks up from pollution in the atmosphere.) And recently, 39 nations signed an agreement that bans oil exploration and mining in Antarctica for the next 50 years.

• **Nations band together to form larger communities.** The nations of Europe, for example, have formed the European Community (EC). Member nations have agreed not to charge one another taxes on goods that are traded among EC nations. People from any EC nation may travel to any other EC nation without special permission.

• **Nations work together for human rights.** Black people in South Africa were being treated very badly, for example. Because of this, many other countries stopped trading with the nation of South Africa.

People of the world, no matter what country they come from, share many of the same goals. They want to do what is right. People can be patriots, yet they can band together to make the world a better place for all the people from all nations.

Helping the homeless and the poor to build their own homes is one way to express your patriotism.

People from all over the world are sworn in every year as new
citizens of the United States.

# 9

## A NEW LAND TO CALL HOME

**MANY PEOPLE ARE BORN IN ONE COUNTRY,** but at some time during their lives, they move to another country. When people leave the country where they were born, we say they *emigrate* from that country. People who are new to a country are called *immigrants*.

There are many reasons that people choose to emigrate. Sometimes life is hard for them in the country where they were born. There might not be enough food for everyone. People often leave their homelands because they are not allowed to practice their religious faith. Sometimes people flee because the government of their country is harsh, and they are in danger of being killed. And sometimes people leave their homeland in search of a better life for their families.

Most immigrants don't forget the land and people they have left behind. They often continue to speak their native language at home even though they have learned the language of their new country. Many immigrant families take great care to teach their children about the customs and traditions of the people of the "old country." Children of immigrants may grow up feeling as if they belong to two nations, their old one and their new one.

Are you new to the country where you live? If you are, you probably feel pride in your family's roots. But you are also probably eager to become a citizen of the new land that is your home. In most countries, immigrants must study and learn about their new land before they can become citizens. Once they do become citizens, they share all the rights and responsibilities that other citizens have in their nation. When people become new citizens, they promise to take on the duties of citizenship, such as voting and paying taxes. They may even be called on to fight for their nation in time of war.

If you are a native-born citizen, you can help new citizens who have come to your country. You can reach out to them in welcome. You can respect their traditions and learn from them. You can work together with them to make your country a better place for all. Then perhaps our new citizens will want to be new patriots, too.

# PATRIOTISM AND YOU

**WHAT CAN YOU DO FOR YOUR COUNTRY?** You don't have to be a famous leader or a soldier to be a patriot. You don't even have to be an adult. There are some things that you can do at any age no matter where you live or work.

### You can show respect for your country.

You can stand up when the national anthem plays or when the flag goes by. You can say the pledge of allegiance to the flag. You can show that you care about your country by doing things like keeping it clean. By your example, others may learn respect for their country, too.

You can protest and still be patriotic. Peaceful protest is a way to
call attention to something you think is important, and to ask for
change.

**You can do the things your country expects of you.**

You can obey the laws of your country. You can serve on a jury. You can pay taxes. You can serve in the army if your country calls you. But if you don't believe in war and you choose not to serve, you can still call yourself a patriot. You can serve your country in many other ways.

**You can expect your leaders to be patriots.**

You help to choose the leaders of your country when you vote. You should expect those leaders to care about your country as much as you do. You should expect your leaders to do things that will be good for the country. If you don't think your leaders are doing the right things you should speak out by writing letters to newspapers or addressing a town meeting. And you can vote against a leader who is not doing a good job. You may even choose to become a leader yourself.

**You can try to do things to make your country a better place to live.**

A group of American patriots got together in the late 1980s. Two of them were famous, but most of them were ordinary citizens. The famous Americans were the former President Jimmy Carter and his wife, the former First Lady Roslyn Carter. The group formed an organization called "Habitat for Humanity."

**Chapter Ten**

Joining the Peace Corps allows people to be patriotic by helping people in other countries.

**"My fellow Americans, ask not what your country can do for you; ask what you can do for your country."**
*—John F. Kennedy*

---

Habitat for Humanity helps people build their own homes or rebuild rundown or abandoned housing units. The poor or homeless people have no money to pay for the homes, but they help build them. This kind of help is called "sweat equity." Habitat workers and the people whose houses are being built work together to get the job done. In this way, Habitat for Humanity helps their country by helping others to help themselves.

### You can represent your country well.

If you travel to another country the people you meet there usually know what country you are from. They decide how they feel about your country by the way you act. If you are nasty, they may believe that most of the people from your country are nasty. If you are polite, they may believe that most of the people from your country are polite.

### You can stand up for your country.

If someone is saying bad things about your country, you should not keep quiet. You should speak up. You should say how you feel about your country. Explain to the other person why you think your country is great even if it is not perfect. If you don't, you are letting your country down.

Remember, your country is your home. It is the land you love.

# Glossary—*Explaining New Words*

**acid rain**  Rain that contains harmful chemicals it picks up from the pollution in the atmosphere.

**anthem**  A song of praise, especially for a country. Every country has an anthem.

**commit**  To do or perform. The person who *commits* the crime is the person who does the crime.

**Communism**  A form of government in which there is one political party. This party usually controls business and the things people are allowed to do and say.

**emigrate**  To move from one country to settle permanently in another.

**famine**  A serious shortage of food which creates widespread hunger.

**immigrant**  A person who has moved from one country to settle permanently in another.

**independence**  Freedom, often from someone or something. Mexico fought for its *independence* from Spain, for example.

**inspire**  To fill with courage or hope. A coach can *inspire* a team to win.

**loyalty**  The feeling that you will stick by one person or a group of people, no matter what.

**Olympic Games**  An international sporting event held every four years until 1992. After 1992, the Winter Olympics will be held in 1994 and every fourth year thereafter. The Summer Olympics will be held in 1996 and every four years thereafter. Athletes from all over the world compete in the Olympic Games. The games are named for some games that were held in Greece thousands of years ago.

**organization**  A number of persons united for some purpose or work.

**republic**  In the former Soviet Union, a division or part of the nation. The Soviet Union had 15 republics until the collapse of Communism in 1991. The Baltic republics—Lithuania, Latvia, and Estonia—were the first three republics to break away and become separate nations.

---

**respect** To show consideration for a person or thing.

**revolution** A war in which people try to end the rule of the government. In the American *Revolution,* the Americans ended the rule of the English king over America.

**"sweat equity"** Helping to build or fix a house instead of paying for it with money.

**symbol** Something or someone that stands for something else. A flag is a *symbol* of a country.

# *For Further Reading*

Allen, Kenneth. *Fighting Men and Their Uniforms.* New York: Grossett & Dunlap, 1971, 74 pages. This colorful book shows the uniforms of fighting men of many countries. It also tells the stories of the men who wore the uniforms.

Bryant, Adam. *Canada: Good Neighbor to the World.* Minneapolis: Dillon, 1987, 192 pages. This book explains what it means to be a citizen and patriot of Canada.

Clyne, Patricia Edwards. *Patriots in Petticoats.* New York: Dodd, Mead and Co., 1976, 140 pages. This book tells the stories of 17 women who were American patriots.

Dobler, Lavinia and Edgar A. Toppin. *Pioneers and Patriots: The Lives of Six Negroes of the Revolutionary Era.* Garden City, New York: Zenith Books, Doubleday & Company, Inc., 1900, 115 pages. This book tells the story of Phyllis Wheatley and five other important black Americans, including Benjamin Banneker.

Johnson, Linda Carlson. *Our National Symbols.* Brookfield, Connecticut: The Millbrook Press, 1992, 48 pages. In this book you will learn the story of the symbols of America and why they are important.

Nottridge, Harold. *Joan of Arc.* New York: The Bookwright Press, 1988, 30 pages. This is the story of Joan of Arc, the young woman who led the French army and was later burned at the stake. The story is told in pictures as well as words.

Spies, Karen. *Our National Holidays.* Brookfield, Connecticut: The Millbrook Press, 1992, 48 pages. This book explains the many national holidays that celebrate America's past, present and future.

# INDEX

### About the Author

Linda Carlson Johnson taught junior-high and high-school English for nine years before embarking on a second career in publishing. After reporting for daily and weekly newspapers, she became an editor for a publisher of childen's literature. She has written for *Weekly Reader*, the children's newspaper, and *Know Your World, Extra*, a special education periodical for junior-high students. Currently, Ms. Johnson is editing family publications.

### Photo Credits and Acknowledgements

*Cover Photo: Barabra Kirk*
*Pages 2, 8, 10, 12, 20–21, 30, 43, 56, Wide World Photos; pages 15, 17, 32, 54, Charles Waldron; page 22, Industry, Science and Technology Canada; pages 24, 27, The Bettman Archive; pages 36, 39, UPI/Bettman Newsphotos; pages 35, 40, Culver Pictures, Inc; pages 47, 49, 50, Stephanie FitzGerald.*

**Design and Production:** Blackbirch Graphics, Inc.